a pocketful of

RHYME

Imagination for a new generation

2006 Poetry Competition for 7-11 year-olds

YoungWriters

Poems From Manchester

Edited by Annabel Cook

First published in Great Britain in 2007 by:
Young Writers
Remus House
Coltsfoot Drive
Peterborough
PE2 9JX
Telephone: 01733 890066
Website: www.youngwriters.co.uk

SB ISBN 1 84602 756 X

Foreword

Young Writers was established in 1991 and has been passionately devoted to the promotion of reading and writing in children and young adults ever since. The quest continues today. Young Writers remains as committed to the nurturing of poetic and literary talent as ever.

This year's Young Writers competition has proven as vibrant and dynamic as ever and we are delighted to present a showcase of the best poetry from across the UK and in some cases overseas. Each poem has been selected from a wealth of *A Pocketful Of Rhyme* entries before ultimately being published in this, our fourteenth primary school poetry series.

Once again, we have been supremely impressed by the overall quality of the entries we have received. The imagination, energy and creativity which has gone into each young writer's entry made choosing the poems a challenging and often difficult but ultimately hugely rewarding task - the general high standard of the work submitted ensured this opportunity to bring their poetry to a larger appreciative audience.

We sincerely hope you are pleased with this final collection and that you will enjoy *A Pocketful Of Rhyme Poems From Manchester* for many years to come.

Contents

Grania Crookes (9)	37
Sam Morgan Skinner (9)	38
Leah Ambler (9)	39
Samantha Beedle (10)	40
Harriet Martin (9)	41
Jessica Renshaw (9)	42
Louise Beaumont (9)	43
Leif Black (9)	44
Aiden Chiu (9)	45
Ashley Martin (11)	46

Rolls Crescent Primary School

Nathan Ouanes (6)	47
Tionne Williams (6)	48
Shiante Blake (7)	49
Grace Samuel (6)	50
Mohamed Said (7)	51

St Catherine's RC Primary School, Didsbury

Megan Stadnicki & Niamh Sharkey-Milum (8)	52
Justine Keeling & Rachael Keeling	53
Daniel Henderson-Cox (8)	54
Kieran McLaughlin (8) & Felix White	55
Alfie Hall	56
Ella Power (8)	57
Jack Jessé & Nathan Donegan (8)	58
Becky Cullinane & Fiona Taylor (8)	59
Georgia Welsby & Jamie-Anne Rochford	60
Annabel Newbery (10)	61
Isobel West (6)	62
Sean O'Connor (6)	63
Caitlin Samuels (5)	64
Scarlett Hollings (6)	65
Billy Gallagher & Joe Connolly (9)	66
Nicholas McGowan (9)	67
Michael Sheehan & Andrew Finn (9)	68
Isabel Webb & Madeleine Saunders (9)	69
Chloe Hernandez (9)	70
Lucy Williams (10)	71
Fhaye Bousfield & Anna McDonald (9)	72
Luke Walsh (10)	73

Annabel Newbery (10)   74
Ryan Johnson (10)   75
Megan King-Stones (10)   76
Katie-Anne Armstrong (10)   77
Ysabel McGuire (11)   78
Jenny Merrick (10)   79
Stephen Berrington (11)   80
Caitlin Millican (10)   82
Joe Furlong (10)   83
Gemma Collinge (8)   84
Gemma Grobicki (8)   85
Madeleine Healey (8)   86
Georgie Conlan (9)   87
Hannah Cawley (8)   88
Victoria Smyth (8)   89
Kathleen O'Connor (8)   90
Grainne Stagg (8)   91
Briony O'Hagan (8)   92
James D'Souza (8)   93
Gabriel Hollings (8)   94
Max Goddard (8)   95
Georgia Hall   96
Thomas Deasy (10)   97
Danielle McNab (10)   98
Emma Yates   99
Deane David Coughlan   100
Jonathan Morrissey   101
Farrell Armstrong   102
Joe Creedon (10)   103
Autumn Isaac (11)   104
James Clavin (10)   105
Sally Hurst (10)   106
Charlotte McGinnis (10)   107

St George's Central CE Primary School
Nathan Rigby (9)   108
Josef Hampson (9)   109
Kai Ashurst   110
Morgan J Foster (10)   111
Leah Statham (9)   112
Sam Champion (9)   113

St Michael's CE Primary School, Middleton

Beatrice Eileen Leáo Do Prado Wall (10)	156
Jodie Barnett (10)	157
Harry Howard (11)	158
Joseph Thompson (10)	159
Tom Barlow (10)	160
Christian Cumpstay (11)	161
Jessica Orr (10)	162
Chelsea Morris (10)	163
Lauren Waterman (10)	164
Georgina Briggs (10)	165
Scott Howarth (10)	166
Mitchell Robinson (10)	167
Laura Cowen (10)	168
Eve Williams 10)	169
Ellie Williams (10)	170
Ben Crompton (10)	171
Gregory Squibbs (11)	172
Jake Lapping (10)	173
Olivia Dyson (10)	174
Jack Crabtree (9)	175
Lucy Forrest (10)	176
Ben Maycock (9)	177
Jessica Taylor (9)	178
Izzy Robinson (9)	179
Max Kent (9)	180
Lucy Vernon (9)	181
Jessica Eaton (10)	182
Alex Caine (9)	183
Hannah Dalziel (9)	184
William Byers (9)	185
Daniel Norris (9)	186
Kate Linsley (9)	187
Liam Grey (9)	188
Brittany Marrison (9)	189
Simon Hicks (10)	190
Abigail Chesters (9)	191
Phebe Morson (9)	192
Sophie Pegum (9)	193
Chloë Hogg (9)	194
Alec Williams (9)	195
Natalie Bradbury (9)	196

The Poems

Autumn

In the autumn I can see
beautiful squirrels at my knee.

In the autumn I can hear
the wind wafting across my ear.

In the autumn I can smell
wet moss on a church bell.

In the autumn I can touch
crunchy leaves very much.

In the autumn I can taste
the air when I'm in a race.

David Brown (10)
Baguley Hall Primary School

That Warm Feeling

Autumn is the time for conkers
Their spiky coats sharp and rough
Acorns dancing in the trees
Squirrels collecting food for their long sleep
Hunting around without a peep.

That warm feeling is great
It makes me feel fine
All the adults are drinking whisky and wine
The leaves are falling on the floor
The owls are hooting for evermore.

I can feel the wind in my face
In this lovely place
There is a lot of space
To relax and be calm
That lovely autumn feeling
That warm autumn feeling
That calm autumn feeling
Makes me feel happy!

Jade Louise Egan (10)
Baguley Hall Primary School

Autumn

In the autumn I can see red foxes
lurking in the dark back garden and leaves falling.

In the autumn I can hear people
walking past my house stomping on twigs.

In the autumn I can feel dry crackling leaves
that have fallen on the floor.

In the autumn I can smell delicious soup being made.

In the autumn I can taste blazing hot food.

Dylan Winstanley (10)
Baguley Hall Primary School

Autumn Is Here

Autumn is here once again!
Robins singing to wake us up.
Brown, green, purple and orange leaves
skipping across the grass.
Trees blowing calmly, scattering
and leaves blowing off them.
Wake up, rise and shine, autumn is all mine.
Go out, breathe warmly and misty.
Smell freshly raked grass.
Feel wind rushing past your face.
Wet grass on your legs.

Jenny Disley (10)
Baguley Hall Primary School

In The Autumn . . .

In the autumn I can see,
Peaceful birds flying over me.
The wind is blowing hedges and trees,
In the autumn you spot no bees.
Blackberries grow upon the hedges,
Frost and mist lying on the ledges.

Autumn brings coldness and mist,
This is when we have the harvest.

In the autumn I can hear
The wind blowing in my ear.
The conkers are falling with a *thud,*
Have they hit Little Red Riding Hood?
I can hear the crunchy leaves,
Like a swarm of buzzing bees.

Autumn brings coldness and mist,
This is when we have the harvest.

Tia Newell-Ellis (10)
Baguley Hall Primary School

The Robin Chirps

With a big bold beak and a ruffled red chest,
The robin chirps a cheerful song.
Autumn is here and the berries are ripe,
The church bells go ding-dong.

The squirrels are getting married,
With their beautiful bushy tails.
The party has just started
And their marriage is ready to sail.

With a big bold beak and a ruffled red chest,
The robin chirps a cheerful song.

Autumn is here and the berries are ripe,
Goodnight says autumn.

Rebecca Wilding (10)
Baguley Hall Primary School

The Autumn

In autumn I can hear
The rabbits scurrying away to their homes

In autumn I can taste
The hot chocolate sliding down my throat

In autumn I can smell
The bonfires raising as large as an elephant

In the autumn I touch the prickly conker's shell.

Thomas Minty (11)
Baguley Hall Primary School

Autumn

In the autumn I can see
Squirrels scattering their way up a tree
There are children playing conker war
That's all I can see.

In the autumn I can hear
Dogs barking and the crunch of the leaves
And twigs and enormous trees going swish swish.

In the autumn I can smell
Treacle toffee and I can smell wet moss on a log
I can smell the breeze in the air.

In the autumn I can touch
Rock solid conkers very much.

In the autumn I can taste
Toffee apple on my face.

Sam Buckley (10)
Baguley Hall Primary School

Autumn

In the autumn I can see
Squirrels and birds and lots of leaves on the floor,
I can see the rain smashing on the door.
I can see rain going by.
I can see the dark clouds in the sky.

In the autumn I can hear
Branches rattling because of the wind.
I can hear children saying trick or treat
And people giving them something to eat.

In the autumn I can feel
The big bag of sweets in my hand,
I can feel the rain smashing across the land.

In the autumn I can smell
Warm food coming from windows,
I can smell moss coming from wet trees.

Josh Marsh (10)
Baguley Hall Primary School

Autumn

In autumn I can see
Trees blowing, tree by tree.
Leaves, brown and green,
Not many daffodils seen.
The leaves are falling fast,
The sun doesn't seem to last.
Some rainy showers,
Only a few flowers.
Autumn, autumn, autumn.

Kim Nixon (11)
Baguley Hall Primary School

Autumn

Touch the leaves on the trees.
Look at the buzzing bees.

Autumn is full of acorns,
The yellow, red and orange leaves,
On the trees almost falling off.

Feel the wind blowing you away,
Wet grass growing on your legs.
Don't forget the wet drops dropping
Off the trees onto your heads,
Autumn is full of acorns.

Shauna Smith (10)
Baguley Hall Primary School

Autumn

Orange leaves falling,
Orange, red and brown,
Falling to the ground,
Making that crunching sound,
Wintertime is nearly here, just take a look around.

Acorns under every tree,
Sometimes conkers too
And when you look up at the sky it isn't always blue.

When you walk outside your door you hear birds chirping
And when you're drinking a nice warm drink
You will end up slurping.

In autumn there is Hallowe'en, harvest and Bonfire Night
And with these winds you can even fly a kite.

Orange leaves falling,
Orange, red and brown,
Falling to the ground,
Making that crunching sound,
Wintertime is nearly here, just take a look around.

Michaela Jackson (10)
Baguley Hall Primary School

All About Autumn

At autumn I can see
Leaves falling off the trees and the birds sing.
All the children collect conkers,
Then they start going bonkers.
On Hallowe'en the children scream,
Lots of children do trick or treating,
Then they say trick or treat smell my feet,
Give me something nice to eat.
At Bonfire Night we can see fireworks twisting and twirling,
People starting to use sparkles to write their names!

Chantelle Evans (11)
Baguley Hall Primary School

Autumn Is Here

Autumn, autumn, autumn,
Autumn is here at last again,
Leaves falling from trees,
Birds singing as they fly in the sky,
Children laughing as the sun shines,
Children eating cherry pies.

Jenna Garner (10)
Baguley Hall Primary School

Autumn

The sky is blue, the sun is bright,
The leaves of autumn come out,
What a beautiful sight.
Conkers drop, acorns fall,
Squirrels come out to collect them all.
Birds sing, trees sway side to side,
Berries are red, some berries are blue,
Yellow and lots more too.
The grass is green, the sun is bright,
Now that's all about autumn's nature life.

Shona Macdonald (10)
Baguley Hall Primary School

Autumn Is The Place To Be . . .

Autumn is when the leaves fall off the trees,
Some creatures and insects hide away as honeybees.
The winds come out at autumn and give us all a big blow,
Birds don't usually hide away especially a crow.
You can't run away from autumn because it's a nice place to be,
In autumn I can see trees blowing tree by tree.

In autumn all I can see is leaves coming after me,
Autumn is for love and peace, I wouldn't rather be in Greece.
The sun can never last because summer goes so fast,
A bit of a rainy shower, only one flower,
Autumn is a place to be only for you and me.

Jessica Bailey (10)
Baguley Hall Primary School

Autumn

In the autumn I can see
the crunchy leaves on the floor.
In the autumn I can hear
the birds singing and flapping their wings.

In the autumn I can smell
the bonfires outside my door.
In the autumn I can touch
the warm covers in the night.
In autumn I can taste
the treacle toffee after my tea.

And finally it's winter.

Syd Bendelow (10)
Baguley Hall Primary School

Friendship

Boom, boom
He's a mate
Boom, boom
He's great
Boom, boom
He's funny
Boom, boom
He's fast
I hope our friendship lasts.

Keelan McIntosh (9)
Highfield Primary School

A Rainbow

Hello, I'm a rainbow
I give a little shine
I glimmer in the sunlight
I am really bright
I come and go
I have lots of colours
I come when the sun is out
And it rains
There's no doubt I like colours
I'm a rainbow
Can you see me?

Christopher Wagstaff (9)
Highfield Primary School

This Is Just To Say

I have eaten
The chocolates
That were hidden
In the sofa

And which
You were probably
Going to save
For your sleepover

Forgive me
They were caramelly
And so delicious
I wish you were here.

Natasha Gilpin (10)
Highfield Primary School

Rock Star

I want to be a rock star
I want to have a flashy car
I want to have my own fashion line
I want my house made of pine
I want to have a swimming pool
I want to be so totally cool
I want to own a glitz guitar
I want to be a rock star
I want to own some ring-tailed sloths
I want to see some downtown goths
I want to be on MTV
I want the music just for me
I want to be in the band Green Day
I've heard they get some wicked pay
I want my hand imprinted on tar
I want to be a rock star!

Thea McQuaid Jones & Grace Winstanley (10)
Highfield Primary School

I Wanna Be A Superstar

I want to drive a funky car
I want to be a fairy
I want to be hairy
I want to have a lot of money
I want to be like a bunny
I want to be a superstar
I wanna buy a big shop
I want to drink all the pop.

Jordan Buckley (10)
Highfield Primary School

I Wanna Be A Superstar!

I wanna be a superstar!
I wanna drive an awesome car!

I wanna own a private plane!
I wanna come here again!

I wanna sing just for you!
I wanna be with you but I have the flu!

I wanna chew a string from a guitar!
I wanna be a superstar!

I wanna have a massive house!
I wanna eat loads of grout!

I wanna have loads of sweets!
I wanna eat every day of the week!

I wanna have the colour red!
I wanna go to my bed!

I wanna play the guitar
I wanna be a superstar!

Bethanie Smith (10)
Highfield Primary School

Bear

I am brown with shiny fur.
Whenever I see her it brings back memories.
I am unhappy through my glassy eyes,
I have seen her grow old and sick
And it is very hurtful to me.
The little speaker in my body runs dry
But I try to keep on going,
She sits with me as we are so lonely and sad.
I will never leave her and I will always be close.
Life is short but I try to make the most of it
And so I will sit here until her and my time
Comes to an end.

Olivia Murphy (10)
Highfield Primary School

I Wanna Get Out

I wanna get out,
I wanna be about,
I wanna go to different places,
I wanna do lots of races,
I wanna scream and shout,
I wanna get out.
I wanna be a jungle kid,
I wanna skid,
I wanna sway from side to side,
I wanna climb up the mount,
Oh please, I wanna get out.

Emma Nightingale (10)
Highfield Primary School

Frostbite

I looked outside my window,
There was frost,
Then the next day that frost was lost.
The day after that I looked out of my window,
It was clear, then I realised the frost was here.
I wonder if I can eat some ice,
But then I figured it wouldn't be nice.
I looked at my window, it had icicles on
And then the next day they were all gone.
I wrapped myself up and stepped out of the door,
There was a blast of snow that made frost on the floor.
I gingerly walked onto the crunchy snow
And I was starting to wish it would never go.
Then three weeks later the coldness had gone
And when I looked outside there was but none.

Holly Henderson & Kya Buller-Frew (10)
Highfield Primary School

Castle

I am made out of stone and I'm very immense,
I have built round me a lake and a fence.
Inside me live lots of rich and royal people,
Their bad prisoners are locked in the steeple.
All I have to look at is the blue sky,
It's ever so boring being so high.
Every day seems to go so slow,
I wish it would have more of a flow.
I'm not that intelligent, but know how to stand straight,
So because of that, I have to watch my weight.
All I can say is I do my best,
But, most of the time I need a *rest!*

Ellie Williams (10)
Highfield Primary School

I Wanna Be A Superstar!

I wanna be a superstar!
I wanna drive a groovy car,
I wanna be a VIP,
I wanna have people notice me,
I wanna have my name in lights,
I wanna turn wrongs to rights,
I wanna have a flash guitar,
I wanna be a superstar
I wanna have a pair of rings,
I wanna have them from all the kings,
I wanna be dead cool,
I wanna have a massive pool,
I wanna travel back in time,
I wanna try Coke and lime,
I wanna lotta caviar,
I wanna be a superstar!

Chloé Morley (10)
Highfield Primary School

I Wanna Be A Superstar

I wanna be a superstar,
I wanna travel far and far.
I wanna drive the coolest car,
I wanna go on a jet,
I wanna be a private vet.
I wanna live far away,
I wanna be famous anyway.
I wanna go different places,
I wanna do fantastic races.
I wanna be a superstar,
I wanna drive a fantastic car.
I wanna travel to Mars and back,
I wanna hide money in a sack.
I wanna have a red guitar,
I wanna be a superstar.

Holli Landing (10)
Highfield Primary School

Superstar!

I wanna be a superstar!
I wanna own a club and bar,
I wanna have my name in lights,
I wanna have a ball at night,
I wanna sign autographs,
I wanna sell my grubby flat,
I wanna thrash a flash guitar,
I wanna be a superstar!
I wanna own a million pounds,
I wanna circus with loopy clowns,
I wanna have a first class seat
On the plane to Wannapete,
I wanna have a dressing room so neat,
I wanna be in a lucky dip,
I wanna be the one who gets picked,
I wanna drive a massive car,
I wanna be a superstar!

Katia Elise Duffy (10)
Highfield Primary School

I Wanna Be A Superstar

I want to be a superstar.
I want to be in the rock band.
I want to be on the rock land.
I want to have a rock guitar.
I want a big yellow car.
I want to have a great big drum.

I want to be a good boy.
I want to race a fast car.
I want to play football.
I want to be a good football player.
I want to own a big Hummer.
I want to have a big broom.
I want to be a big wrestler.

Jordan Ambler
Highfield Primary School

This Is Just To Say

I have eaten
The whole bar
Of Galaxy chocolate
From the fridge

And which
You were probably
Saving for after
Dinner

Forgive me
It was delicious
So creamy
And so mouth-watering.

Niamh Bailey (10)
Highfield Primary School

Butterfly

I'm bright and colourful,
I make you feel happy,
I eat yummy green leaves,
I live in your garden.

I have delicate wings
That fly super fast,
I love to flutter through the trees,
I'm extremely pretty.

I'm a little bit shy,
So I won't come too near,
But, my bright colours give me away,
So you'll come too close and I'll fly away.

Jodie May (9)
Highfield Primary School

Guinea Pig

I'm fluffy and fast,
I'm a vegetarian,
I'm always there when you're feeling down,
People say I feel like cotton wool.

I live in a house, I'm a pet,
I'm always nosing around,
I'm sweet and friendly
And never feel down.

I squeak like an alarm
When I'm hungry.

Rachel Carr (9)
Highfield Primary School

Nightmare

I'm a nightmare,
I'm a people killer,
I'm a black car crusher,
Mmm! The taste of crushed cars,
I've got heads on the walls,
I only come out at night,
Another one *oops.*
Another *yesss!*
I've got another one on the wall,
Oh I forgot, you're my next victim.
Faster than light, a human killer.

Kristos Kastrinos (9)
Highfield Primary School

The Tardis

We spin past time
We save the world
We go the speed of light
We travel through time
We look at the time vortex.
We die.

Jake Ribas (9)
Highfield Primary School

Dolphin

I leap like a rainbow
I look really beautiful,

My tail sparkling with glitter
My crystal blue eyes

I jump over the waves
I shine in the sun's rays

My speed of light
My pink diamond tail

I shimmer like the sun
I take up all day

My job is to jump
My long eyelashes

Yes I'm a dolphin!

Grania Crookes (9)
Highfield Primary School

Pig

Sticky brown saddle,
Smooth snorting bacon,
Pink ham rounded,
Tastes of bacon,
Smelly in the slippy mud,
Brown chocolate pig.

Sam Morgan Skinner (9)
Highfield Primary School

Dolphin

A curved creature.
A deep diver.
A human saver.
A sea creature.
A shark killer.
A sea twirler.
A sunset shadow.
A fin turner.
A yo-yo jumper.
A dolphin.

Leah Ambler (9)
Highfield Primary School

My Best Friend

A girl,
A princess,
Bright and beautiful,
Cares for me,
Always there for me,
Helps me get out of
Tremendous trouble.

Samantha Beedle (10)
Highfield Primary School

My Imaginary Dream

I go upstairs and lie in my bed,
Knowing I'm going to have the same unreal dream.

It's like a chocolaty world,
It's sweet syrup tasting.

Its dark atmosphere,
Its gates stand there in secret.

In dark, cold, windy weather,
Then it watches people pass by,
As they do they look at the chocolaty pie.
He tries to stop people pass,
But as he cannot speak they just
Pass, pass, pass.

Harriet Martin (9)
Highfield Primary School

Teddy Bears

I'm cute and fluffy,
I'm golden brown,
I have big black eyes,
I try to warn and tell you things,
But you don't hear.
At night the teddies have a ball,
Until our legs get tired and we fall.
We even eat your food,
But in the morning the food is back,
It's like magic in a box,
But we have to be aware of the time,
So we look at one of the clocks,
But now you leave me in a box,
It's dark and warm in here,
I watch you play from time to time,
But now I have a fear,
You'll leave me here forever,
Bye-bye! (Sniff)

Jessica Renshaw (9)
Highfield Primary School

Dolphin

A dolphin
Goes side to side
Swooping left and right
He is soft
He is fast
And whenever
You see him take a picture
Or you can see him on a boat
He is clever
He jumps through hoops
And does tricks
And I dive and swoop in and out of water
He is a sea swooper
It's a beautiful dolphin.

Louise Beaumont (9)
Highfield Primary School

An Evil Ostrich

A human eater,
A furry monster,
A scary lookout
Comes your way.
Every hour,
Every day,
When he comes
And sets eyes on you,
Then you know
Just what to do.

Leif Black (9)
Highfield Primary School

Pikachu

It's cute, it's electric
it's fuzzy but not
like an Exeggcute
He's smaller than a wall
and he can't roar.
He's yellow, he's brown
and looks like a marshmallow.

Aiden Chiu (9)
Highfield Primary School

Superstar

I want to be a superstar
I want to drive a bling-bling car
I want to be really lucky
I want to have a rubber ducky
I want to have a plasma TV
I want to have a pool table just for me
I want to have Chinese curry
With my rubber ducky!

Ashley Martin (11)
Highfield Primary School

The Hardest Thing To Do In The World

The hardest thing to do in the world is . . .
Get on a plane, especially when there is thunder and lightning,
And when there is a big queue.

Nathan Ouanes (6)
Rolls Crescent Primary School

The Hardest Thing To Do In The World

The hardest thing to do in the world is . . .
To try not to cry, especially when you are sad
And you're angry,
And your mum tells you to stop.

Tionne Williams (6)
Rolls Crescent Primary School

The Hardest Thing To Do In The World

The hardest thing to do in the world is . . .
To catch the moon,
Especially when it's night
And the lights are out
And you have no torch
And you are on your own
And you are scared
And you can hear scary noises
And you are tired of walking.

Shiante Blake (7)
Rolls Crescent Primary School

The Hardest Thing To Do In The World

The hardest thing to do in the world is . . .
To climb a mountain, especially when it is snowing
And the snow is really rough
And the mountain is dry
And the wind is swaying side to side.

Grace Samuel (6)
Rolls Crescent Primary School

The Hardest Thing To Do In The World

The hardest thing to do in the world is . . .
To climb up a mountain, especially when it is raining and it's windy
And the storm comes
And the moon is shining
And the mountain is gold.

Mohamed Said (7)
Rolls Crescent Primary School

I Wish

I wish I was popular and had loads of friends.
I wish I was always happy.
I wish my childhood would never end.

I wish I was clever and always in a good mood.
I wish I had a big house and a massive garden too.
I wish I had nice clothes and lots and lots of food.

I wish I had a family that didn't always row.
I wish I never hurt myself or felt ill.
I wish I had a cat that always went *miaow!*

I wish . . .

Megan Stadnicki & Niamh Sharkey-Milum (8)
St Catherine's RC Primary School, Didsbury

Christmas Horror

There I was on Christmas Eve
The tree was shining bright.
The doorbell rang, I opened it up
And heard a bang.
I screamed and turned
And saw them there
The ghosts of Christmas Eve.
All I remember was lying there on the floor
With a tear of Christmas horror
And from that day on I never enjoyed again
Christmas!

Justine Keeling & Rachael Keeling
St Catherine's RC Primary School, Didsbury

The Man From

The man from Spain had a great pain.
The man from Brazil had a very bad chill.
The man from Brussels had big muscles.
The man from Asia had a laser.
The man from Rome lost his way home.
The man from Norway got stuck in the doorway.
The man from France liked to sing and dance.

Daniel Henderson-Cox (8)
St Catherine's RC Primary School, Didsbury

There Once Was A Man

There once was a man who came from Mars
And he loved to eat chocolate bars.

There once was a man who came from Earth
Who called his baby, Baby Birth.

There once was a man who came from Brazil
And he had a fish with a very bad gill.

There once was a man called Doctor Who
And he needed the loo at hal-past two.

There once was a man who was very fat
And he ended up getting a pet bat.

Kieran McLaughlin (8) & Felix White
St Catherine's RC Primary School, Didsbury

Class Names

A is for Alfie who's the cleverest in the class.
B is for Becky, she wears glasses.
C is for Christopher, he is very cheeky.
D is for Darragh, he's good at football.
E is for Emily, she is very smart.
F is for Felix, he is annoying.
G is for Georgia who's the funniest in the class.

Alfie Hall
St Catherine's RC Primary School, Didsbury

The Haunted House

One Hallowe'en I walked down the road,
I stepped into a house that was full of ghosts!
I screamed my head off and ran upstairs
But all there was were three grizzly bears!
So there I was in the wooden bed,
When all of a sudden two scary skeletons were tickling my head!
I ran to the kitchen, where my mum was stitching
And out of nowhere popped four little witches!
So I found out it was only a nightmare
But it also gave me a very big . . .
Scare!

Ella Power (8)
St Catherine's RC Primary School, Didsbury

Christmas

Santa lives in the North Pole.
He comes down for Christmas
And gives little children their presents.
He eats his mince pie
And gives the carrots to Rudolf and off they fly.

Jack Jessé & Nathan Donegan (8)
St Catherine's RC Primary School, Didsbury

Alphabet Poem (Food)

B is for burgers that taste so good.

F is for flavoured chocolate ice cream.

M that reminds me of mud.

J is for jam that I put on my toast.

N is for noodles, so stringy I boast.

R is for roast dinner that I have every Sunday.

T is for the tasty food that we all love.

G is for goodies that I have for a treat.

Becky Cullinane & Fiona Taylor (8)
St Catherine's RC Primary School, Didsbury

Friend-Ship

On the Friend-ship we're all friends.
On the Friend-ship we have hens.

In the Friend-ship we play games.
In the Friend-ship we're called by our names.

Outside the Friend-ship we look through the roof.
Outside the Friend-ship we hear our dogs go *'woof'*.

Georgia Welsby & Jamie-Anne Rochford
St Catherine's RC Primary School, Didsbury

Annabel's Kennings

Crisp - eater
Dog - stroker
Animal - lover
Flower - planter
Bed - sleeper
Game – player
Baby - sitter
TV - watcher
Apple - picker
Door - user
Ice cream - eater
Chocolate - lover.

Annabel Newbery (10)
St Catherine's RC Primary School, Didsbury

When I Grow Up . . .

When I grow up
I want to be
A famous painter
With her own gallery.

When I grow up
I want to be
A mermaid swimming
Through the seven seas.

When I grow up
I want to be
The prettiest princess
For the whole world to see.

Isobel West (6)
St Catherine's RC Primary School, Didsbury

When I Grow Up . . .

When I grow up
I want to be
Swimming in the deep
Deep, deep sea.

When I grow up
I want to be . . .
The fastest and
The tallest runner.

When I grow up
I want to be
The best diver in the class
And in the galaxy.

Sean O'Connor (6)
St Catherine's RC Primary School, Didsbury

When I Grow Up

When I grow up
I want to be
A tiny little flea.

When I grow up
I want to be
A person who has
Lots and lots of parties.

When I grow up
I want to be
A fish that likes to swim
In the deep blue sea.

Caitlin Samuels (5)
St Catherine's RC Primary School, Didsbury

When I Grow Up

When I grow up
I want to be
A mum who has a baby.

When I grow up
I want to be
The best at my own numeracy.

When I grow up
I want to be
The best at sailing
Over the seven seas.

Scarlett Hollings (6)
St Catherine's RC Primary School, Didsbury

Bob's Job

There was a lad called Bob
Who wanted an ordinary job.
He didn't fancy being a bus driver
Or a scuba-diver.

He started to weep
And fell into a deep sleep,
Then gave up looking
And remembered cooking
And that was
His job from then on.

Billy Gallagher & Joe Connolly (9)
St Catherine's RC Primary School, Didsbury

Astro Pig

I live on a farm and I have a pig.
But this pig is like no other.
He takes off into space
And lands on his moon base
Where he has robots galore.

He has a blaster at his side
Although he can't reach it
Because he is rather wide
But he still beats up baddies
Really good.

He takes off to Mars
And puts baddies behind space bars
And makes it back to moon base
All in time for lunch.

He gets on his ship
And takes a nice dip
In his personal hot tub.

He took me to Jupiter
And it was rather super
To meet all the little space people.

Now my pig's stopped his space adventures
And he's come back to Earth
Now hopefully he'll wallow in the dirt.

Nicholas McGowan (9)
St Catherine's RC Primary School, Didsbury

My Cat's A Thief

My cat's a thief, he eats roast beef.
He robs houses and gets caught by the chief.
My cat's a thief, he bullies the police.
He stole a fleece from a cat with fleas
He got put behind bars
After he blew up Mars.

Michael Sheehan & Andrew Finn (9)
St Catherine's RC Primary School, Didsbury

My Sister's Crazier Than You

My sister's crazier than you,
You should see the things she will do.
She will eat mushy peas with a tin of baked beans
That's only one of the things that she'll do.

My sister's crazier than you,
This is reason number two.
I don't know how but she'll ride a cow
Whilst sitting in a canoe
And that's reason number two.

My sister's crazier than you,
Here's reason number three
Why my sister's crazier than me.
She went to sea on a tiny green pea
And that's reason number three.

My sister's crazier than you,
She may be crazier than you and me
But she's the best sister that could ever be.

Isabel Webb & Madeleine Saunders (9)
St Catherine's RC Primary School, Didsbury

The Light Is So Bright

The light is so bright
It shines through the night.

I was thinking of the sun
But my mum gave me a fright
So I said, 'Mum, how come the light is so bright?'

And she said, 'It's supposed to be bright
Because it's a light.'
Oh! So now I know why light is so bright!

Chloe Hernandez (9)
St Catherine's RC Primary School, Didsbury

Dog Kennings

Tail - flicker
Fur - licker
Bone - scratcher
Cat - catcher
Ball - hitter
Meal - eater
Moon - howler
Mud - roller
Flea - catcher
Master - sneezer
Crazy - king
Mad - Max.

Lucy Williams (10)
St Catherine's RC Primary School, Didsbury

I Often Daydream

When the teacher's talking I often go into a dream,
Her lips move so fast they're like a machine.
I go into a far-off land,
Where there is often a band.
Everyone wears purple silk
And I get a glass of milk.
Then I hear a faint noise - *blah, blah, blah!*
Then the voice starts talking about a star.
I open my eyes
I see my teacher not at all surprised.
'You'll end up in Hell!'
My teacher says with a yell.

Fhaye Bousfield & Anna McDonald (9)
St Catherine's RC Primary School, Didsbury

James

James is a burning flame
Exploring down the hall.

He is a joking boy, sitting in a deckchair
On a hot summer's day.

He is a marine,
Shooting people down in a laser quest.

James is a stormy day
With his umbrella tangled in the air.

He is a pair of tight jeans
Covered in chains and rips.

He is an athlete
Swinging on a large wooden chair.

He is a comedian
Doing a stage dive.

James is a pile of chocolate
That a whole group of athletes couldn't finish in one day.

Luke Walsh (10)
St Catherine's RC Primary School, Didsbury

If My Thoughts Took Shape

If my noisy thoughts took shape,
They would be a marching band
Going around the world.

If my wonderful thoughts took shape,
They would be a very big shopping centre
All the way across England.

If my scary thoughts took shape,
They would be Hallowe'en every day
All over the world.

If my frightened thoughts took shape,
They would be like all the scary books I've read
Coming to life.

If my wicked thoughts took shape,
They would make me
The queen of the world.

If my heroic thoughts took shape,
They would save everyone
From bad things that happen.

If my sunny thoughts took shape,
They would be jumping over the waves
Making sandcastles in the sand.

If my sad thoughts took shape,
They would be on an island
I'd be all by myself.

Annabel Newbery (10)
St Catherine's RC Primary School, Didsbury

Thoughts . . .

If my scary thoughts took place,
I would be gone without a trace.

If my evil thoughts took place,
I would be king of all this place.

If my imaginative thoughts took shape,
This place would be a chocolate factory.

If my furious thoughts took place,
They would be the Devil's blazing face.

If my romantic thoughts took shape,
They would be a red rose, as red as lips
And a table for two.

If my confusing thoughts took place,
I would be stuck with a poem in school.

If my never-ending thoughts took shape,
This world would be a better place.

Ryan Johnson (10)
St Catherine's RC Primary School, Didsbury

My Kennings Poem

Rattle - shaker
Earth - quaker
Can't - speak
But - unique
Milk - drinker
Clever - thinker
Toy - lover
Happy - mother
Crawling - around
Making - sound.

Megan King-Stones (10)
St Catherine's RC Primary School, Didsbury

If My Thoughts Took Shape . . .

If my longing thoughts took shape,
They would be a horse or pony.

If my frightful thoughts took shape,
They would be a barrel of snakes.

If my loving thoughts took shape,
They would be a stable at home.

If my upsetting thoughts took shape,
They would be a friend dying.

If my exciting thoughts took shape,
They would be a friend on holiday with me.

If my disastrous thoughts took shape,
They would be a bad mark on my SATs.

If my pretty thought took shape,
They would be a fancy dress ball.

If my selfish thoughts took shape.
I wouldn't tell a soul!

Katie-Anne Armstrong (10)
St Catherine's RC Primary School, Didsbury

If My Thoughts Took Shape

If my romantic thoughts took shape,
They would be like a candle burning in the dark.

If my shameful thoughts took shape,
They would be like a person jumping off a cliff.

If my funny thoughts took shape,
They would be like a cow jumping over the moon.

If my lazy thoughts took shape,
They would be like someone sitting in a chair slouching
                                    and watching TV.

If my quiet thoughts took shape,
They would be like water trickling down a river.

If my thoughtful thoughts took shape,
They would be like giving a flower to a fabulous friend.

If my scary thoughts took shape,
They would be like a gigantic tarantula crawling over me.

Ysabel McGuire (11)
St Catherine's RC Primary School, Didsbury

If My Thoughts

If my evil thoughts took shape,
They would be like a devil screaming.

If my noisy thoughts took shape,
They would have my music on full blast.

If my scary thoughts took shape,
They would be scared like a mouse
            that was being caught by a snake.

If my happy thoughts took shape,
They would be like a person buying a whole shop.

If my hurtful thoughts took shape,
They would be crying like a person who has been
                arrested for more than 18 years.

If my crazy thoughts took shape,
They would laugh like a hyena that was laughing so much.

If my sad thoughts took shape,
They would be like a person who has fallen over in hospital.

If my proud thoughts to shape,
They would be me passing my SATs.

Jenny Merrick (10)
St Catherine's RC Primary School, Didsbury

If My Thoughts Took Shape

If my evil thoughts took shape,
They would be a defenceless whale
Being harpooned for meat.

If my lazy thoughts took shape,
They would be a chair in which
You'd sit all day.

If my happy thoughts took shape,
They would be a person
Helping everyone they met.

If my furious thoughts took shape,
They would be an asteroid
Blowing up the galaxy.

If my confusing thoughts took shape,
They would be millions of people
Wandering aimlessly around for shelter.

If my quiet thoughts took shape,
They would be a non-existing wind
Whistling away.

If my frightening thoughts took shape,
They would be billions of corpses with no eyes,
And blood everywhere wandering towards me.

If my noisy thoughts took shape,
They would be every choir
In the world screaming.

If my imaginative thoughts took shape,
They would be a laboratory
Which had remade dinosaurs.

If my romantic thoughts took shape,
They would be two people
On a date kissing each other.

If my secret thoughts took shape,
They would be a secret
That could destroy anything.

If my never-ending thoughts took shape,
We would explore strange new life and civilisations
And boldly go where no one has gone before.

Stephen Berrington (11)
St Catherine's RC Primary School, Didsbury

If My Thoughts Took Shape

If my happy thoughts took shape,
They would be on holiday by the beach
Looking over at the sea.

If my helpful thoughts took shape,
They would be helping people
With no money or no homes to go to.

If my funny thoughts took shape,
They would be my friends making me laugh.

If my frightening thoughts took shape,
They would be on a roller coaster
And holding a giant spider!

If my angry thoughts took shape,
They would be me shouting and crying.

If my romantic thoughts took shape,
They would be a picnic for two
And a romantic meal.

If my disgusting thoughts took shape,
They would be eating oranges
And Brussels sprouts.

If my cross thoughts took shape,
They would be my mum blaming me
For something my dad has done.

Caitlin Millican (10)
St Catherine's RC Primary School, Didsbury

Wayne Rooney

Rooney is the strong red sensation of England.
He is a footballer in winter breaking through the
icy mountains.
He is the king of Old Trafford, cheering on the crowd.
Rooney is an angry storm, rippling the back of the net
with lightning strikes.
He is the red shirt of England and United.
He is a living wardrobe with power and pace.
He is the best goal on 'Match of the Day' every time.
Rooney is a football and Shrek cake for his birthday.

Joe Furlong (10)
St Catherine's RC Primary School, Didsbury

My Teacher And Me

My teacher likes maths.
My teacher likes English.
My teacher likes all sorts of things
But oh she likes art the best.
I really do like English.
I really do like maths
But when it comes to art
Oh I have a blast.

Gemma Collinge (8)
St Catherine's RC Primary School, Didsbury

Flowers

Flowers are beautiful, flowers smell nice.
If you mess with them they might die.

Flowers sit in a vase,
If you don't water them they will drift off.

Flower, flower, be back in an hour
And buy some lovely things.

For you and me will have some tea
And something to eat.

Gemma Grobicki (8)
St Catherine's RC Primary School, Didsbury

Christmas Time

On Christmas Eve when I was in bed,
a jingle of bells came into my head.
I went downstairs with a skip and a hop,
and heard a mighty, mighty plop.
For there was a man in a red gown and a hood,
and all of his redness was covered in soot.
So I reacted to this, 'Oh it's Saint Nick,'
for there were many names I could pick.
So he said, 'Happy New Year,'
and all the room filled with love and great cheer.

Madeleine Healey (8)
St Catherine's RC Primary School, Didsbury

Autumn

Autumn, autumn, autumn leaves,
Falling from the autumn trees,
Drifting in the autumn breeze,
I really like the autumn leaves.

Autumn leaves swing and sway,
On the branches of the trees all day.
When autumn day is done,
A fiery, red, big, wide sun,
Goes down and down and down,
Until the world stops spinning round
And when it's dim and dark,
The leaves hustle and bustle
In the park.

I like jumping in autumn leaves,
With piles high from massive trees!
They try and fly right away,
But I still play night and day.

Georgie Conlan (9)
St Catherine's RC Primary School, Didsbury

Mums

Some mums are mean
Some mums are lean
But not my mum.
My mum's a queen.

Some mums shout
Some mums doubt
But not my mum
My mum just finds things out.

Some mums moan
Some mums groan
But not my mum.
She's always on the phone.

Hannah Cawley (8)
St Catherine's RC Primary School, Didsbury

Sizes And Prizes

All shapes and sizes
Makes lots of prizes, twist them, turn them
They will still be prizes
Turn them twist them
They will still be sizes
Up, down, left and right
See the prizes!
You will get a fright.

Don't enter you will never get a prize
Doesn't matter what size!

Victoria Smyth (8)
St Catherine's RC Primary School, Didsbury

Christmas

At Christmas it seems magical,
I think about bells jingling,
And the snow outside.

At Christmas it seems happy,
I think about people smiling,
And how lucky we are.

At Christmas it seems beautiful,
I think about lights,
And people everywhere.

But most of all,
I think
Will I ever see Saint Nick?

Kathleen O'Connor (8)
St Catherine's RC Primary School, Didsbury

When I Feel

When I feel that winter air
I feel like I could fly.
When I feel that spring air
I feel like I could go to Heaven.
When I feel that summer air
I feel like an angel.
When I feel that autumn air
I feel like I could fall asleep.

Grainne Stagg (8)
St Catherine's RC Primary School, Didsbury

My Teacher And My Bunny

My teacher rode a donkey,
My teacher rode a horse,
My teacher rode a dinosaur
And she fell off the horse.

My bunny hopped to London,
My bunny danced a jig,
My bunny ate some grass,
My bunny went to bed
And jumped off the shed.

My teacher ran to London,
My teacher screamed in bed,
My teacher ate a worm
And balanced a jug on her head.

My bunny has a hutch,
My bunny has a pen,
My bunny has a lot of food
And also has a hen.

My teacher met my bunny,
She told him he was cute,
She told him he was beautiful
And would like to take him home.

Now my bunny wasn't having this,
He already had a home,
He told my teacher all of this
And then he said, 'Goodbye!'

My bunny came home to me,
My bunny had a cuddle,
My bunny had a shepherd's pie,
And then he said, 'Hi!'

Briony O'Hagan (8)
St Catherine's RC Primary School, Didsbury

Me And My Mummy

Me and my mummy went walking
Me and my mummy saw sweets
Me and my mummy had money
So we got a sweet.

Me and my mummy went jogging
Me and my mummy saw clothes
Me and my mummy had money
So we got loads.

Me and my mummy went running
Me and my mummy saw a house
Me and my mummy had money
So we got a house.

Me and my mummy wet walking
Me and my mummy saw a donkey
Me and my mummy had money
So we got a donkey.

James D'Souza (8)
St Catherine's RC Primary School, Didsbury

Sweets

I love sweets
They're such a treat.
When I hear the word treat
I dream about a sweet
Never mind toffee, chocolate and marshmallow.

I love a treat
Such as a sweet
You just can't beat a sweet
It's so good to eat. I love a sweet
It's a treat you just can't beat.

I love a sweet!

Gabriel Hollings (8)
St Catherine's RC Primary School, Didsbury

The Little People Of The Night

In hundreds you may kill,
Still you will find there's thousands still,
For they hide away in the dark,
Then you get a painful bite,
For they have an extreme appetite,
They have their love for mothers,
Fathers and sisters too!

Max Goddard (8)
St Catherine's RC Primary School, Didsbury

Wouldn't It Be Funny?

Wouldn't it be funny if I had a fat tummy?
Wouldn't it be funny if I was a mummy?
Wouldn't it be funny if I had a bunny?
What do you think about that?

Wouldn't it be funny if I had no money?
Wouldn't it be funny if I was a mummy that goes boo?
Wouldn't it be funny if I had no tummy?
What do you think about that?

Georgia Hall
St Catherine's RC Primary School, Didsbury

If I Won The Lottery

If I won the lottery, I would buy a house,
If I won the lottery, I would have a pet mouse.

If I won the lottery, I would have a horse,
If I won the lottery, I'd be poor no more.

If I won the lottery, I would buy a car,
If I won the lottery, I'd be rich by far.

If I won the lottery, I would buy a truck,
But I haven't won the lottery and for me that is bad luck.

Thomas Deasy (10)
St Catherine's RC Primary School, Didsbury

A Kennings Poem

Floor sleeper,
Midnight creeper,
Fur licker,
Tail swisher,
Mouse catcher,
Paw scratcher,
Wall sitter,
Ball hitter,
Lies in the sun,
Loves to have fun.

My cat.

Danielle McNab (10)
St Catherine's RC Primary School, Didsbury

Elvis Presley

Elvis Presley is a warm summer's day.
He is like a red-hot chilli pepper.
He is as stylish as a leather suit.
He is a big blue wave crashing over the rocks in the sea.
He is as hard as an old wooden chair.
He is a cold dark night with a candle burning brightly.
He puts the U into USA - unbelievable.

Emma Yates
St Catherine's RC Primary School, Didsbury

Ronaldo

Ronaldo is a blazing red devil speeding down the pitch roaring
He is as cold as an ice cube
He is as hard as a balcony
He is as hot as red chilli pepper
He is Mr Old Trafford
He is all the reasons racing through each one
He is the blazing hot sun
Ronaldo is as calm as a summer's spring morning
He has the pace.

St Catherine's RC Primary School, Didsbury

Steven Gerrard

Steven Gerrard is a fiery dragon breathing down your neck
He is a red-hot summer's day
He is as strong as a steel metal chair
His feet are on fire on a rainy day
He is the king of the Kop
He is like a red-hot chilli pepper steaming in your face
He is the captain of the mighty Reds
He is the man of a Liverpool shirt
Steven Gerrard is the greatest!

Jonathan Morrissey
St Catherine's RC Primary School, Didsbury

Untitled

Joey Barton is strong as a bullet and blue as the sky
He is as great as Gerrard and funny as a clown
Is blue as furniture, on a bed but is a cover
He is as fierce as a chilli pepper
He is like a Man City top
He is like a football boot when they get bought
He is as hot as a summer day
He is like Blackpool Pleasure Beach
He is as big as a giant
He is as cold as an ice cube.

Farrell Armstrong
St Catherine's RC Primary School, Didsbury

John Terry

John Terry is a bull of stone letting nobody past.
He is a bear in a ferocious blizzard.
He is the bridge in Stamford Bridge always supporting
                                    the other players.
He is all the seasons, playing all the time, whatever happens.
He is as cool as a cucumber.
He is as tough as a wooden stool in a workshop.
He is a helmet, only the toughest of things get past.
He is black and blue giving bruises to everyone he meets on the pitch.
John Terry is the ultimate captain.

Joe Creedon (10)
St Catherine's RC Primary School, Didsbury

Jerry (Out Of Tom And Jerry)

Jerry is as small as a marble as it rolls across the floor.
He is as tough as a hard stool,
He is as soft as silk,
He is as bright as the morning sun,
He is as light as a bird's feather,
He is as red as the bright red Devil.

Jerry is a marble as it rolls across the floor.
He is as small as a baby's sock,
He is as big as a crumb of cheese,
He is as grey as the clouds on a winter's morning,
He is as calm as the Barbados sea.

Autumn Isaac (11)
St Catherine's RC Primary School, Didsbury

Ashley Tisdale

Ashley Tisdale is as graceful as a windy bright morning.
She is sweet as apple pie.
She is a red cunning fox.
Ashley Tisdale puts the L in London and loving.
She is as comforting as a pair of shoes.
She is a hot summer morning.
Ashley Tisdale is as hard as a wooden stool.
Ashley Tisdale *is* the star of the show.

James Clavin (10)
St Catherine's RC Primary School, Didsbury

Kenning Poem

Sweet-eater,
> Nail-biter,
Cat-frightener,
> Toy-snatcher,
Fly-catcher,
> Couch-sitter,
Drops-litter,
> Long-sleeper,
Teddy-keeper,
> Picture-maker,
Family-waker,
> Juice-drinker,
Big-thinker!
. . . My sister.

Sally Hurst (10)
St Catherine's RC Primary School, Didsbury

A Kennings Poem

Basket sleeper,
House creeper,
Ball catcher,
Leg scratcher,
Night howler,
Street fowler,
Tail flicker,
Nose licker,
Ball hitter,
Floor sitter

My dog.

Charlotte McGinnis (10)
St Catherine's RC Primary School, Didsbury

Autumn Is Here

A conker
As round as the sun
As brown as chocolate
And harder than a brick
Autumn is here

A leaf
As smooth as a baby's bum
As wrinkly as Grandma
As red as fire
Autumn is here

A tree
As tall as Big Ben
As thin as a pen
As dark as a swamp
Autumn is here.

Nathan Rigby (9)
St George's Central CE Primary School

Autumn Is Here!

A leaf
As crunchy as a crisp
As soft as skin
As dirty as coal
Autumn is here!

A conker
As round as the sun
As smooth as a baby
As hard as metal
Autumn is here!

A squirrel
As grey as Grandad's hair
As red as blood
As small as a mouse
Autumn is here!

Josef Hampson (9)
St George's Central CE Primary School

Autumn Is Here

The rain
As heavy as a brick
As clear as the sky
As wet as water
Autumn is here.

Kai Ashurst
St George's Central CE Primary School

Autumn Is Here

Autumn, autumn, one of the best seasons
And I don't have to give any reasons
Autumn is the season when the leaves turn brown
Autumn is the season when conkers fall down
Autumn is the season when the leaves float down
Autumn is the season when people might frown.

Morgan J Foster (10)
St George's Central CE Primary School

Autumn Is Here

An acorn
as hard as a brick
as smooth as a whiteboard
as oval as a face

A leaf
as brown as mud
as red as an apple
as crunchy as a crisp

A tree
as tall as Big Ben
as long as a piece of string
as green as grass

Autumn is here.

Leah Statham (9)
St George's Central CE Primary School

Autumn

A utumn leaves are falling red, yellow and brown,
U nder the horse chestnut kids collect conkers.
T he deciduous trees are losing leaves,
U nder the oak tree are lots of acorns.
M ums are out for Hallowe'en sweets,
N ear the end of autumn it starts to show
                    a sign that winter is near.

Sam Champion (9)
St George's Central CE Primary School

Autumn Poem

Autumn days when the trees stand bare
And the autumn leaves lie over there
Evergreens still stand there
With their leaves and branches blowing everywhere
We put on our wellies and big thick coats
And go to the park but not in the dark
Squirrels get ready to hibernate
They go collecting nuts with their mates
Conkers and acorns there they lie
Pine cones and branches we see as we go by
Looking through the window of the bus
We see the colours all around us
We all know autumn is here
And that Christmas will soon be here.

Katie Macafee (9)
St George's Central CE Primary School

Autumn Is Here

A twig,
as long as a piece of string,
as thick as a book,
as spiky as a conker's shell.
Autumn is here.

The rain,
as heavy as a brick,
as round as a football,
as clear as a crystal.
Autumn is here.

A leaf,
as red as fire,
as spiky as a stick,
as crisp as a crisp.
Autumn is here.

Megan Wright (9)
St George's Central CE Primary School

Autumn Is Here

A twig,
as thin as a pencil,
as rough as a wall,
as brown as mud.
Autumn is here.

A squirrel,
as fluffy as a teddy,
as fast as lightning,
as short as a shoe.
Autumn is here

A conker,
as smooth as a tissue,
as round as a ball,
as brown as a twig.
Autumn is here.

Lauren Toone (9)
St George's Central CE Primary School

Autumn

Autumn leaves are changing
every single colour.
Autumn leaves are fading
because it is getting colder.

Trees are starting to look bare.
There is moss everywhere
and leaves are falling through the air.
You know Jack Frost is there.

Animals are hibernating
they are wrapping up tight.
Birds are migrating
having a lovely flight.

The days are getting darker now
earlier at night.
It is autumn now
so all of us wrap up tight.

Leah Pendlebury (9)
St George's Central CE Primary School

Autumn

A utumn leaves are falling down to the ground
U nder the trees fallen leaves
T he leaves fall slowly to the ground
U nder the tree orange and yellow leaves on the ground
M adness! Leaves falling from trees
N asty leaves are dark brown and light brown leaves.

Jamie Roberts (9)
St George's Central CE Primary School

Autumn Is Here

A squirrel,
as bushy as a shoe brush,
as cute as a teddy,
as fast as lightning.
Autumn is here.

A branch,
as lumpy as a rock,
as brown as mud,
as spiky as a conker shell.
Autumn is here.

The rain,
as loud as thunder,
as clear as crystal,
as cold as snow.
Autumn is here.

Carenza Reece (9)
St George's Central CE Primary School

Autumn Is Here

The days are short, the nights are long,
the colourful leaves fall to the ground.
A carpet of colour covers the street
crunching and rustling under my feet.

Children out playing having lots of fun,
it's cold and windy and there is no more sun.
Collecting acorns and conkers, pulling up leaves
the branches are empty on the trees.

A great time of year, Hallowe'en and Bonfire Night
ghosts and witches give us a fright.
Pumpkins light the windows as we do trick or treat,
it's lots of fun, presents and tasty things to eat.

For the animals, it's time to hide away,
the birds fly south, it's too cold to stay.
We stay inside snuggled up warm,
soon the snow will cover the lawn.

Jack Toone (8)
St George's Central CE Primary School

Autumn Is Here

Autumn days, when everyone says
The nights are longer than the days

Autumn is here
Let's give a cheer
Scream and shout
Autumn is here

Little animals go away for the winter
Cos autumn is ten times colder
Birds fly north for the winter.

Autumn is here . . .

We see acorns and plenty of conkers
Mum and Dad go really bonkers
We play in all the conkers

Autumn is here . . .

Alice Lummis-Green (10)
St George's Central CE Primary School

Autumn Time

Crunchy leaves
underfoot whimpering and
calling in the slush.

A squirrel glides in the sky,
a majestic hound
makes a sound.

A beastly bug sits
in the mud, a curly
branch has a dance.

A hedgehog does
hibernate, but at the
night before he stays
up late.

A catalogue to
make me an
autumn day.

David Borbash (10)
St George's Central CE Primary School

The Sun

A burning ball
A fire call
A circle in the universe.

Warms you up
And keeps you good
Keeps you brown
When you are in the town.

Veronkia Jelisejeva (10)
St George's Central CE Primary School

A Little Seed

A little seed
A tiny weed

A mini trunk
A load of junk

A lot of sticks
As strong as bricks

As swaying flopper
A great hopper

Now it's time for leaves to fall
To bounce on the floor like a ball

A catalogue to make me
A tree.

Robert Mann (10)
St George's Central CE Primary School

A Hard Bone

A hard bone
A big moan

A bad clash
A crazy lash
A precious land
A sound like a band

A loss of antelope
A painful thing to cope

A catalogue
To make me
A reindeer.

Alex Bell (10)
St George's Central CE Primary School

A Snake Shiver

A slithery slime
A creature in prime

A venom spitter
A pouncing sitter

A hiding waiter
A non dater

A spotty line
A killer in time

A people eater
A nasty creature

A catalogue to make me
A snake.

Luke Unsworth (10)
St George's Central CE Primary School

The Wind

A blowing breeze
A nasty sneeze

A howling sound
A dog's pound

No one sees this howling sound
But only hear this dreadful pound

The wind calms down
While you're outside in your dressing gown

Now it's a restful sound!
The wind!

Kareena Talbot (11)
St George's Central CE Primary School

Sun

The light blazing all over the world
a big ball of fire in the sky
orange and yellow
it makes you smile
once in a while
when it appears you want to say goodbye.

Ryan Oxley (10)
St George's Central CE Primary School

What Is The Wind?

The wind is like a howling ghost
That flew into a post

What is the wind?
The wind is like a waterfall
That is very tall

What is the wind?
The wind is like a fight
That happens in the night

What is the wind?
The wind is like a squeaky mouse
That does not fit in a house.

Shannon Schofield (11)
St George's Central CE Primary School

Autumn Is Here

A leaf,
as crunchy as Yorkshire pudding,
as smooth as water,
as rough as a hedgehog.
Autumn is here.

A conker,
as solid as a rock,
as brown as mud,
as round as the sun.
Autumn is here.

A tree,
as tall as Blackpool tower,
as thick as a wallet,
as rough as a wavy sea.
Autumn is here.

Michael Valentine (9)
St George's Central CE Primary School

Autumn Is Here

The rain
like a big bass drum
as heavy as a big rock
as clear as glass.
Autumn is here.

A twig
as thin as a pen
as light as a feather
as brown as brown paper.
Autumn is here.

A leaf
as small as a hand
as thin as a ruler
as light as a twig.
Autumn is here.

Megan Holt (8)
St George's Central CE Primary School

Autumn Is Here

A tree,
As tall as a mountain,
As wavy as my mum's afro,
As big as the planet.

A leaf,
As red as a crunchy leaf,
As crunchy as an ice cream cone,
As rough as a rock.

A conker,
As shiny as the sun,
As round as a football,
As brown as hot chocolate.

Bethany Paige Pavitt (9)
St George's Central CE Primary School

Autumn

Autumn leaves floating down.
Trees changing colours green to brown.
The autumn breeze rustles them around.

Leaves of red and brown and gold.
Autumn leaves floating down.
Hedgehogs roll up and go to sleep.
Little children through frosty windows peep.

Types of birds fly south for the winter.
In autumn you will get a splinter.
The squirrels bury nuts for the winter then go to sleep.
The trees look skinny because leaves fall off.
Autumn is faded and winter is here.

Jonathan Chadwick (8)
St George's Central CE Primary School

Autumn

Autumn is here it's my favourite time of year
Red, yellow, orange and brown
All the trees' leaves fall down
Children going to the park
All wrapped up in their hats, gloves and scarves
Walking through the crunching leaves
We kick them, throw them, more please
On Hallowe'en it is a frightening night
We dress up and give people a fright
Soon it will be Bonfire Night
Fireworks and bonfires are set alight.

Connor James Nixon (8)
St George's Central CE Primary School

Autumn Days

The trees were swaying
as children were playing
in the autumn breeze

The children ran around and around
until the ground began to freeze

Leaves were falling all around
landing softly on the ground

Me and my brother have a competition
to collect the most conkers
our mum and dad think we're bonkers

The autumn day is at a close
so we all have to go to bed for a doze.

Joseph Hudson (8)
St George's Central CE Primary School

Autumn

A utumn days get shorter each and every week
U nder the trees all the leaves lie
T rees stand with bare branches
U p the trees squirrels go to hibernate
M ost turn central heating on as it gets colder
N ow we know *autumn* is here.

Bethany Hodcroft (9)
St George's Central CE Primary School

Autumn

A lways in autumn
U nder the leaves
T he squirrels will stay dry
U mbrellas not needed
M y time goes short
N ever do days go longer in autumn.

Adam Toone (9)
St George's Central CE Primary School

Autumn

A conker,
as round as the sun
as smooth as a table,
as brown as mud.
Autumn is here.

The rain,
as heavy as a brick,
as loud as screaming,
as many as stars.
Autumn is here.

A squirrel,
as fast as lightning,
as small as a spider,
claws as sharp as a sword.
Autumn is here.

A branch,
as still as air,
as thick as ice cream,
as rough as dry mud.
Autumn is here.

Daniel Partington (9)
St George's Central CE Primary School

Autumn Is Here

A leaf
as thin as a person
as long as a hair
as stripey as a curtain
as brown as brown paint.
Autumn is here.

As fast as a cheetah
as hairy as a hair
as tall as a twig
as cute as a dog.
Autumn is here.

As strong as a brick
as clear as a house
as long as a drop
as short as a leaf.
Autumn is here.

Courtney Chambers (9)
St George's Central CE Primary School

Autumn Is Here

A squirrel was eating a chestnut
U p the squirrel goes
T rees are losing their leaves in autumn
U mbrellas decorate the town
M um is making hot cocoa
N ana is making warm clothes.

Ellie Hennedy (8)
St George's Central CE Primary School

Autumn Is Here

A conker
As round as a football,
As hard as a brick,
As small as a tennis ball,
As bouncy as a bed,
As fat as a log.

Jonathan Chadwick (8)
St George's Central CE Primary School

Autumn Days

Conkers crashing to the ground
Makes a lovely crispy sound
Autumn is here
It's my favourite time of year
Red, yellow, orange and brown
All the leaves off the trees falling down
Autumn is here
It's my favourite time of year
Nearly Hallowe'en, my favourite time of autumn.

Milly Lewis (9)
St George's Central CE Primary School

A Tiny Egg

a tiny egg
a slimy head

a long tail
a hissing wail

a scaly skin
a bony chin

a forked tongue
ever so long

a glistening eye
a little sly

the venom means
a killing machine

a catalogue to make
me a snake!

Lauren Aspinall (11)
St George's Central CE Primary School

The Sun

A hot ball
A burning wall.

A big light
a blinding sight.

A high height
it's stuck tight.

A big balloon
like the moon.

A scorching fire
don't go any higher.

A flying bonfire
is my desire.

A catalogue to make
me the sun.

Cara Davies (10)
St George's Central CE Primary School

The Snail

Slimy and slow,
slithery and cold,
come out of your shell
and have some dinner.

Slimy and slow
slithery and cold
leave your trail
along the road.

Slimy and slow
slithery and cold
up the kerb you go
while your trail goes.

Slimy and slow
slithery and cold
go back in your shell
and sleep very slow.

Beth Sutherland (10)
St George's Central CE Primary School

King's War

The king on his throne
eating a bone

Swords clashing
waves crashing

Men dying
women crying

Houses burning
rivers churning

A catalogue to make
me a soldier.

Mathew George Smith (10)
St George's Central CE Primary School

A Great Flyer

A great flyer
A fake dyer

A flying gonner
A kamikaze bomber

A beak fighter
An eater at night

A nut lover
A good mother

A bullet hater
A slick dater

A catalogue to make me
an *owl*.

Brandon Roche (11)
St George's Central CE Primary School

Slithering Snake

Slithering through the deserts
not knowing where to go
he slithers around and sleeps
then the wind comes and he goes.

Slithering snake scatters through the sand dunes.
The wind blows then he pops his head
out of the sand *boo!*
but then he pops his head back in.

Ryan Little (10)
St George's Central CE Primary School

An Autumn Day

Trees swaying
children playing

Magpies calling
squirrels mauling

Acorns dropping
conkers popping

Leaves changing
rivers raging

Horses trotting
roots rotting

A peaceful way
for an autumn day.

Luke Hudson (10)
St George's Central CE Primary School

Winter Days

The winter is so cold
The wind is so bold
The snow is so white
And we have a snowball fight
A warm crackling fire to warm my heart's desire.

Ben Piggott (10)
St George's Central CE Primary School

The Sun

Through the summer the sun's awake,
going to autumn it's getting cold,
who knows where the sun has gone,
the sun has never been heard or told.

We are coming to winter day by day,
getting on our hats, gloves and scarves,
where has that sun gone?
I wonder how cold it is on Mars?

Rachael Molyneaux (10)
St George's Central CE Primary School

Autumn Is Here

A branch
as long as a car,
as brown as brown paint,
as rough as a brick.
Autumn is here.

Jake Hupton (8)
St George's Central CE Primary School

Autumn Is Here

I bent my knees to catch
the colourful leaves falling from the trees.
Autumn is here.
Autumn is there.
Autumn is everywhere.
I stretched up high,
to look at the cloudy sky.
Autumn is here.
Autumn is there.
Autumn is everywhere.
I sat down on the ground
to look at the red berries
I had found.
Autumn is here.
Autumn is there.
Autumn is everywhere.

Millie Talbot (8)
St George's Central CE Primary School

Autumn Poem

Autumn leaves are falling
squirrels and badgers calling
badgers hide in burrows
squirrels climb up willows
autumn nights are dark
no more going to the park
orange and yellow leaves fall from trees
hedgehogs hide in leaves
summer flowers have gone away
but evergreens are here to stay
certain animals must now sleep
until spring's alarm clock goes bleep.

Jamie Roberts (10)
St George's Central CE Primary School

An Autumn Poem

Autumn is here but once a year
The sun is low and the trees are bare
It once was warm but now is cold
The leaves are falling
And they are dry and old
The wind blows around
Lifting the leaves from the ground
The leaves change from green to red
And as you play they fall on your head
We pick up leaves and make a pile
The sun is up and we all smile
Autumn is a wonderful time of year.

Jamie Shaw (9)
St George's Central CE Primary School

The Old Castle

Black night spreads the gloomy scene
As the misty moon shines with spirits
The screeching bats glide through the air,
Wind howling through the trees.

Will the princess be trapped?
Will her knight arrive
Or not survive
The way of the dragon?

Crumbling walls, no man can fix.
Chains rattle with fear
Enemies once attacked but we believed not.
Now bricked-in windows
No light to be seen.

King's spies ascended the wall
To attack.
Walk in . . .
Walk in . . .
All is mysterious within.

Beatrice Eileen Leáo Do Prado Wall (10)
St Michael's CE Primary School, Middleton

The Old Castle

I watch with patience,
Bats and rats creep around me,
People come and go,
They never stay for long here,
I'm just too cold and heartless.

Finger-like branches twist and twirl,
Bats swoop in every dark turret,
Debris lies everywhere,
Cobwebs cover the ancient royal suite,
Infestations of rats in every passageway,
Lit only by moonlight.

Jodie Barnett (10)
St Michael's CE Primary School, Middleton

The Old Castle

Windows, empty and alone,
From the top window
We think someone watches us,
But no one is there.

Crumbling and falling down
From old age,
The roof tries to hold together.
Not succeeding.

Harry Howard (11)
St Michael's CE Primary School, Middleton

The Old Castle

Sun sinks down triggering rainfall,
Night bats come out,
Strange wind blowing,
Cold crumbling door,
Once arrows flew
Hitting the castle.

Joseph Thompson (10)
St Michael's CE Primary School, Middleton

The Old Castle

The howling wind,
Sweeping the leaves
Off their feet.

Crumbling bricks,
Rotting away.
Where knights
Once shot from.

Pitch-black bats circling
This dark, gloomy castle.

Mist drifts upon the castle
Over knights who once fought here.

Tom Barlow (10)
St Michael's CE Primary School, Middleton

The Old Castle

Hills guard the castle,
Grass and reeds are soldiers here.
Windows are smashed
Where birds and bats fly.

Ivy grows high up the walls.
Rocks fall down into the moat.
The moon shines down onto the castle.
Birds rest on the turrets.
Mist covers the entrance.

Rusty chains hold the drawbridge up.
Walls caving in.

Christian Cumpstay (11)
St Michael's CE Primary School, Middleton

The Old Castle

A milky moon watches
Once-bloody battles,
Now people in cars
And children with phones.

Mossy green ripples
Splash about the silky moat.
Once chains pulled the heavy drawbridge
Up and down; now they lie still.

The old wall crumbling, now so weak!
Birds swoop up and down and in and out.
A once-steady entrance is now crumbling stones.

The beautiful moon gleams in and out of the tall turrets,
The still wind speaks.
When the gate comes down on knights
Many an arrow is shot.

Jessica Orr (10)
St Michael's CE Primary School, Middleton

The Old Castle

Birds swoop up and down,
Swirling round and round,
Flapping wings all around
The old castle.

Mysterious windows, different shapes,
Old and rusty
Never break
The old castle.

Lightning strikes the castle,
Yellow and bright,
Shines in my eyes,
The old castle.

Tall and freaky
Is the castle.
Old and ruined;
The old castle.

Chelsea Morris (10)
St Michael's CE Primary School, Middleton

The Old Castle

The wind throws the sounds of ancient cannonballs
Around the battered walls; the orchard surrounding,
The gate rusting and crumbling;
The drawbridge is falling apart.

Mist clears and comes back at night,
Prisoners are left in the gloomy cells
Ropes left with skeletons hanging,
A feast still there waiting and waiting.

But all of these horrid things can be good,
For the grass is green,
The trees are growing wildly,
But no one forgets the castle . . .

Where men once died with honour.

Lauren Waterman (10)
St Michael's CE Primary School, Middleton

The Old Castle

The moon shines in the dark night,
A bird's call echoing;
Deep, calm water gently sways in the wind,
Rusty and old are the windows,
Bricks fall one after another,
Chains rattle together
In the dark night.

Long ago soldiers attacked
In front of the castle.
Dark, abandoned . . .
The bridge creaks when stepped upon
In the dark night.

Georgina Briggs (10)
St Michael's CE Primary School, Middleton

The Old Castle

Mist lurks upon the top of the castle,
It is hard to get rid of.
Mountains shadow the green, gloomy water,
Leading to the monstrous portcullis.

Grass no longer grows here,
Since cannons burnt it.
The long weeds sway in the wind,
Stopped rigid, not moving.

Scott Howarth (10)
St Michael's CE Primary School, Middleton

The Castle

Behind the mist,
Under the clouds
Stands the grey castle.
There the cobwebs hang.
The rusty chains hold up the bridge.
Ghosts haunt the castle,
Gravestones on guard.
Myths about the castle still told.
The moat from sky-blue to grass-green.
Bats fly round and round.

Mitchell Robinson (10)
St Michael's CE Primary School, Middleton

The Old Castle

The drawbridge is old and creaking,
A deep moat surrounds the castle,
Vines twist up the wall,
It's creating an eerie scene.

Soldiers once came to battle at the castle,
Flags once swayed high in the wind,
Windows are now unclean.

Mist surrounds the gloomy castle,
Trees wave their scrawny fingers,
The gate is old and rusty,
However, it is still jagged.

Hills are the backdrop for the once-proud castle,
Clouds circle around the milky moon,
Crows and ravens swoop into the turrets
Calling in the dead of night.

Laura Cowen (10)
St Michael's CE Primary School, Middleton

The Lonely Castle

A lonely, gloomy castle,
With filth, dirt and mould,
Stands on a hillside;
Enemies must have battled here once.
Ancient turrets crumble,
Bats and hawks surround the castle.
The misty moon heaps unhappiness
Onto the shadowy walls.
Its cellar is full of rats;
People say that it's haunted.
Do not go near!

Eve Williams 10)
St Michael's CE Primary School, Middleton

The Old Castle

Swirling through the sky, the mist it shall be;
The door inside is not to see;
Birds and bats hide in cracks
Their cries are not to be heard,
Yet echoing through the sky.

Chains of sterling shall never break,
But now the broken windows are there for travellers
As they call in the dead of night.

Ellie Williams (10)
St Michael's CE Primary School, Middleton

The Old Castle

Ancient turrets crumble,
Pitch-black bats and dark ravens swoop down
And land on the turrets looking for food.

Rust covers the portcullis,
Sharp points closing,
One long and one short, but they go down.

Dark water covers the castle,
Swirling and swaying;
Weeds lie in the moat.

Ben Crompton (10)
St Michael's CE Primary School, Middleton

The Old Castle

Wind howls and echoes in the mist,
There on the ground is some sort of list.

It's said to be of the people who died here.

The slime upon the castle walls,
The slime just drips off and falls.

As I enter the castle walls,
Rocks fall shaped like balls.

Gregory Squibbs (11)
St Michael's CE Primary School, Middleton

The Old Castle

Ancient walls crumble,
Dry blood stains on the walls,
The milky moon lights up the sky,
Bats glide over the turrets,
Weeds rustle in the wind,
Moors in the background,
Rusty chains hold up the bridge,
Walls with holes in, made by cannons.
Raindrops falling silently,
Clouds circle the moon,
Insects live inside the castle.

Jake Lapping (10)
St Michael's CE Primary School, Middleton

The Old Castle

Wind howls in the darkness of night
Sending an evil message.
Birds are whistling beside the wind,
Bats making their exit out of the castle.

Into the castle
I make my way.
Doors slam shut;
No way out.

All the wooden windows
Cry for help.
Rats come back in,
No way out.

Running away from the bats,
Hiding from them,
The door flies open;
I'm free!

Olivia Dyson (10)
St Michael's CE Primary School, Middleton

Wings

If I had wings
I would smell the salty sea
And the fresh air.

If I had wings
I would touch the rainbow
And find a pot of gold.

If I had wings
I would taste a cloud
As chewy as a marshmallow.

If I had wings
I'd look down at everyone
Like ants and specs of dust.

Jack Crabtree (9)
St Michael's CE Primary School, Middleton

If I Had Wings

If I had wings
I would feel the candyfloss clouds
Sniffing up the lovely scent.

If I had wings
I would touch the rings of Saturn
Looking down in fascination.

If I had wings
I would taste the Milky Way
Dreaming pleasantly.

If I had wings
I would see the people as ants
Looking big and bold.

If I had wings
I would hear the soaring of an eagle
So gracefully.

Lucy Forrest (10)
St Michael's CE Primary School, Middleton

If I Had Wings

If I had wings
I'd scoop a bit of *ow! ow!*
Red-hot sun,
I'd take a bite *yum-yum!*
A bit like chilli pepper.

If I had wings
I'd hear the faint *tweet-tweet,*
Tweet-tweet of the cute
Little fluffy chicks.

If I had wings
I'd smell the sweet smell
Of the fresh air.

If I had wings
I'd touch the clouds
And sleep on them so comfy.

If I had wings
I'd see the beautiful world
Down below.

Ben Maycock (9)
St Michael's CE Primary School, Middleton

If I Had Wings

If I had wings
I would touch the clouds
As soft as candyfloss.

If I had wings
I would watch all the people
And see how small they were.

If I had wings
I would listen to the drips of rain.

If I could fly
I would dream.

Jessica Taylor (9)
St Michael's CE Primary School, Middleton

If I Had Wings

If I had wings
I would fly to the moon
To look down from space.

If I had wings
I would go to the galaxy
To eat all the chocolate.

If I had wings
I would taste
The candyfloss clouds.

If I had wings
I would smell the air,
Tasty and smelly.

If I had wings
I would touch the blue sky
Light blue and sparkly.

If I could fly
I would dream . . .

Izzy Robinson (9)
St Michael's CE Primary School, Middleton

If I Had Wings

If I had wings
I would touch the clouds
To see if they were white cotton candy.

If I had wings
I would gaze upon
The famous capital cities of the world.

If I had wings
I would fly around the world
And be famous.

If I had wings
I would fly to France
And meet my dad.

If I had wings
I would hurtle towards my house
Just in time for bed!

Max Kent (9)
St Michael's CE Primary School, Middleton

If I Had Wings

If I had wings
I would lie on the fluffiest cloud
And sleep for a hundred years.

If I had wings
I would smell the salty sea
And lick my lips as I flew above it.

If I had wings
I would suck all the colours of the rainbow
And suck it up like a colourful sweet.

If I had wings
I would touch the stars
Shining bright and hot as a cooking oven.

If I had wings
I would listen to the birds squabbling
As they go by.

If I had wings
I would taste the clouds
So sweet and soft.

If only I had wings
Life would be so easy
I would fly to school . . .!

Lucy Vernon (9)
St Michael's CE Primary School, Middleton

If I Had Wings

If I had wings,
I would take a bite out of a cloud,
Soft and squishy like a marshmallow.

If I had wings,
I would shoot up to the Milky Way
To see planets twirling round.

If I had wings,
I'd smell every colour of the rainbow,
Leaving its scent on me.

If I had wings,
I'd lie on clouds
Like fluffy pillows.

If I had wings,
I'd fly as high as the sky
Forever . . .

Jessica Eaton (10)
St Michael's CE Primary School, Middleton

If I Had Wings

If I had wings,
I would fly to the top of a mountain
And see the rarest bird and touch it.

If I had wings,
I would swerve through the clouds
And go speeding as fast as a plane.

If I had wings,
I would fly around the world
And smell all of the mountains.

If I had wings,
I would fly into space
To see all the planets.

Alex Caine (9)
St Michael's CE Primary School, Middleton

If I Had Wings

If I had wings,
I would look down on Earth
And see the waves lapping upon the seashore.

If I had wings,
I would see the sun
Breathing its warm breath.

If I had wings,
I would taste the fresh air
From the mountain tops.

If I had wings,
I would touch
The fluffy clouds.

If I had wings,
I would smell the scent
Of the snow-topped mountains.

Hannah Dalziel (9)
St Michael's CE Primary School, Middleton

If I Had Wings

If I had wings,
I'd touch the sky so high.

If I had wings,
I'd help you fly so high.

If I had wings,
I'd say goodbye.

If I had wings,
I'd fly so high.

If I had wings,
I couldn't write.

William Byers (9)
St Michael's CE Primary School, Middleton

If I Had Wings

If I had wings,
I would sit on the highest mountain
So high and cold.

If I had wings,
I would eat spare packs of food
So mouth-watering to eat.

If I had wings,
I would see a brilliant football game
From the sky.

If I had wings,
I would sniff the salty sea
Like fish and chips.

If I had wings,
I would sleep on the fluffiest
Whitest cloud ever.

If only I had wings,
I would fly to school
So easy and quiet . . .

Daniel Norris (9)
St Michael's CE Primary School, Middleton

If I Had Wings

If I had wings,
I would see if I could taste
The candyfloss clouds.

If I had wings,
I would tiptoe
On top of the stars.

If I had wings,
I would try and find
All the planets in the universe.

If I had wings,
I'd drift through
The colours of the rainbow.

Kate Linsley (9)
St Michael's CE Primary School, Middleton

If I Had Wings

If I had wings,
I would fly over the blue ocean,
Proud and strong.

If I had wings,
I would fly through the clouds,
All soft and padded.

If I had wings,
I would fly into space,
Dark and gloomy.

If I had wings,
I would fly in the breezy wind,
Wonderful and refreshing!

Liam Grey (9)
St Michael's CE Primary School, Middleton

If I Had Wings

If I had wings,
I could touch the rainbow
So colourful in the sky.

If I had wings,
I'd like to see the sun
Glistening out in space.

Just if I had wings . . .

If I had wings,
I'd like to keep up with the
            planes in the air,
Zooming like a *rocket!*

Brittany Marrison (9)
St Michael's CE Primary School, Middleton

If I Could Fly

If I could fly,
I would zoom from city to city
In less than one minute flat.

If I could fly,
I would sip the rain from fairy clouds
Like eating candyfloss.

If I could fly,
I would pop out of the blue
Into a warm blue ocean.

If I could fly,
I would play with the eagles
And move swiftly through the air.

If I could fly,
I would socialise in clouds
With litres of water, just for me.

If I could fly,
I would float in space
In a star world.

Simon Hicks (10)
St Michael's CE Primary School, Middleton

If I Had Wings

If I had wings,
I would like to feel the candyfloss clouds
Floating up above.

If I had wings,
I would touch the stars
Twinkling in the sky.

If I had wings,
I would taste the rainbow;
All its different colours.

If I had wings,
I would play with the birds
Flying past me.

If I had wings,
I would sing with the moon
Shining in the sky.

If I had wings,
I would dream so high,
Wondering if it was true . . .

Abigail Chesters (9)
St Michael's CE Primary School, Middleton

If I Had Wings

If I had wings,
I'd touch the white fluffy clouds
As soft as a pillow.

If I had wings,
I'd take a chunk of each colour
From the rainbow.

If I had wings,
I'd hear the sun sizzling
Like a chicken on a barbecue.

If I had wings,
I'd see the highest mountain
Covered in sparkling snow.

If I had wings . . .

It would be
A dream come true!

Phebe Morson (9)
St Michael's CE Primary School, Middleton

If I Had Wings

If I had wings,
I would sleep on
Stars so bright.

If I had wings,
I would smell the smoke
From a barbecue below.

If I had wings,
I would soar
And sit on the highest mountain.

If I had wings,
I would find Heaven
And live there forever . . .

And never go back

If I only had wings!

Sophie Pegum (9)
St Michael's CE Primary School, Middleton

If I Had Wings

If I had wings,
I would touch the end of a star
Delicate and sharp.

If I had wings,
I would kick the Earth
Like a football hard and bouncy.

If I had wings,
I'd cook my bacon on the sun
Hot and sizzling.

If I had wings,
I'd smell the rainbow
Colourful and fruity.

If I had wings,
I would taste the galaxy,
Dark, black and strong.

If only I had wings . . .

Chloë Hogg (9)
St Michael's CE Primary School, Middleton

If I Had Wings

If I had wings,
I would fly up to smell the burning sun
As I was gliding past.

If I had wings,
I would look down on all the specks on Earth
From so far up.

If I had wings,
I could taste the spicy sun
As I flap past.

If I had wings,
I would look at all the galaxies
As I flew through.

If I had wings,
I would fly about madly
Through all the clouds.

I would dream about flying
All over the planets
And the universe . . .

Alec Williams (9)
St Michael's CE Primary School, Middleton

If I Had Wings

If I had wings,
I would touch the fluffy clouds,
Clear and white in the sky.

If I had wings,
I would go and touch a rainbow
To find the pot of gold.

If I had wings
I would swift in and out of the clouds
Feeling the breeze wafting in my face.

If I had wings,
I would sit on the highest mountain
To view a beautiful sight.

If I had wings,
I would say, 'Hi!' to people on planes
And they would wave back.

But only if I had wings . . .

Natalie Bradbury (9)
St Michael's CE Primary School, Middleton

If I Had Wings

If I had wings,
I would glide over the Pacific Ocean
And blaze down.

If I had wings,
I would blaze at the sun
And glide to France.

If I had wings,
I would touch the clouds with my fingertips
To see if they could tickle me.

If I had wings,
I would smell the fresh air
Swooping into my face.

If I had wings,
I would glide over the Indian Ocean
And bounce upon the clouds.

Matthew Atherton (9)
St Michael's CE Primary School, Middleton

If I Had Wings

If I had wings,
I would fly up into the sky
And nibble the candyfloss clouds.

If I had wings,
I could touch the sun
And be far away.

If I had wings,
I would go into space,
I would touch a spaceship.

If I had wings,
I would sit on a soft cloud
And fall asleep on it.

If I had wings,
I would see the stars
And try to touch the corner of one.

If I had wings,
I would listen to the birds.
I wish I could fly!

Faye Coyne (9)
St Michael's CE Primary School, Middleton

If I Had Wings

If I had wings,
I would feel the clouds'
Silver lining.

If I had wings,
I would taste the fluffy sensation
Of the clouds.

If I had wings,
I would smell the red roses' scent
Drifting from below.

If I had wings,
I could see the galaxy
From a different point of view.

If I had wings,
I would fulfil my dream
Of seeing the Northern Lights . . .

If only I had wings.

Nathan Lowe (9)
St Michael's CE Primary School, Middleton

If I Had Wings

If I had wings,
I would touch a bird's beak
Smooth and silky.

If I had wings,
I would sniff the salty air
As I glide over the sea.

If I had wings,
I would taste fluffy clouds
High up in the sky.

If I had wings,
I would stare at people
As I'm in the sky.

I would dream on . . .

Victoria Maher (9)
St Michael's CE Primary School, Middleton

The Old Castle

Ancient walls crumble,
Everywhere candyfloss dust,
Blood splattered in the crumbling towers,
Rusty chains hold up the dirty drawbridge.

Bricks falling apart, crackling,
In and out swoop black bats.
Mist surrounds this gloomy castle,
Old turrets crumble.

Grey bats swoop in and out of the cracked windows,
The cracks in the stone,
Once reflections seen in the moat,
The bloody drawbridge.

Spikes pierce any who dare enter,
Darkness only greets the visitors,
Rust invades the dark chains.
The castle is dead.

Swirling clouds around the misty moon,
The air swooping,
Darkness surrounds the yard,
Visitors come no more.

Lily Hewson (10)
St Michael's CE Primary School, Middleton

The Old Castle

Ancient walls crumble and fall,
Moon shines down like a spotlight,
The gate rusts from the fall of rain,
Chains creak and clang in the gusting of the wind.

Mysterious water travels round the moat,
The drawbridge lies dead over the water,
Wood has broken off and fallen into the moat,
Reeds sway and dance in the gentle breeze.

Warriors lie dead on the ground,
From those battles long ago.
In those times the castle was proud,
Standing behind the army in battle.

Birds swoop down to explore the castle,
Pecking at the walls,
Flying through the softening air,
The wind blows slowly through the gaps in the walls.

Walls cave in because of past times,
When cannonballs thundered through them.
Men used to fight for Scotland,
Flags still swaying in the wind.

Andrew McAslan (10)
St Michael's CE Primary School, Middleton

The Old Castle

Ancient turrets crumbling,
Ebony bats and ruffled ravens
Swooping upon them, so confused.

Where the proud princess once stood
With her shining blonde hair,
Cobwebs have taken her place.

The moat's murky waters,
Lie petrified without a use,
Still hoping soldiers will return.

Long ago, in ancient times,
Enemies once marched with honour
Across the overgrown landscape.

The colossal castle stands
Choked and strangled
By olive-green moss and stems of ivy.

The lonely drawbridge, deserted and still,
Rotting splinter by splinter in the dark,
The ancient dust weighing it down.

The moon envies darkness,
Glistening at night,
With nature's own shining silk.

Inside, the king and his daughter sit side by side,
Still waiting in the darkness,
Not resting, not moving, not even breathing.

Jessica Coburn-Wade   (10)
St Michael's CE Primary School, Middleton

The Old Castle

Mist covers the glistening moon as it shines through the night,
Owls that are searching for food, shriek in delight,
Stars in the night sky, twinkling and bright,
And still I walk on, walk on, walk on.

Deep, dark water churning slowly around,
Mice crawl through the darkness, making hardly a sound,
Wind whistles through the trees, whipping leaves so they dance
on the ground,
And still I walk on, walk on, walk on.

I am just a traveller,
Just a wandering traveller,
Though many things try to divert me
I walk on,
walk on,
walk on.

Jessica Gauld (10)
St Michael's CE Primary School, Middleton